THE FAVOUR

THE CAFOD/CHRISTIAN AID
LENT BOOK 2010

Clare Amos • Michael Campbell-Johnston SJ
Joseph Donders • Ben Edson
Katherine Schexneider • Peter Selby

THE FAVOURABLE TIME

Reflections on the
Scripture Readings for Lent 2010

just one world

First published in Great Britain in 2009 by

CAFOD
Romero Close
Stockwell Road
London SW9 9TY

Christian Aid
35 Lower Marsh
London SE1 7RL

Darton, Longman and Todd Ltd
1 Spencer Court
140-142 Wandsworth High Street
London SW18 4JJ

ISBN 0 232 52780 3

Note: the Hebrew numbering of the Psalms is used. From Psalm 10 to 147 this is ahead of the Greek and Vulgate numbering which is used in some psalters.

Cover photo: Simon Rawles/CAFOD
Cover design: Leigh Hurlock

Text designed and produced by Sandie Boccacci and Judy Linard
Set in 9.5/13pt Palatino
Printed and bound in Great Britain by
Athenaeum Press Ltd, Gateshead, Tyne and Wear

Contents

About the contributors

Clare Amos is Director for Theological Studies in the Anglican Communion Office and Theological consultant for USPG: Anglicans in World Mission. She is a biblical scholar by background, having taught in Jerusalem, Beirut, Cambridge, South London and Kent, and has written extensively on biblical and inter-faith concerns.

Michael Campbell-Johnston SJ is the former Provincial of the British Jesuits and head of the Jesuit Social Justice Secretariat in Rome. He worked in a parish in El Salvador for many years.

Joseph G. Donders, a member of the Missionaries of Africa, is Professor Emeritus in Mission and Cross-cultural Studies at the Washington Theological Union, in Washington DC. He has lectured all over the world and is the author of a number of books.

Ben Edson pioneered and then led Sanctus1 – an emerging church in Manchester city centre – for eight years. He is currently a curate in inner city Manchester, an associate missioner with Fresh Expressions and programmes the worship at Greenbelt Festival.

Katherine Schexneider is an American doctor who recently spent a year in Afghanistan working with local physicians helping them improve their medical practice. She lives and works in the Washington, DC area.

Peter Selby is the President of the National Council for Independent Monitoring Boards. He was previously Bishop of Worcester, Bishop to HM Prisons and a Church Commissioner.

Introduction

Michael Campbell Johnston, one of the contributors to this year's Cafod and Christian Lent Book, writes that when we consider the unfairness and injustice in the world, it is difficult not to feel overwhelmed.

Another writer, Peter Selby, reflects on how cynicism and a sense of powerlessness have been reinforced in recent years by the greed of those responsible for the turmoil in the world's financial markets and by the dishonesty of many members of parliament in the recording of their expenses.

The temptation is to think, this is the way the world is. I am sorry about injustice and greed, but I am powerless to change it. I am only one person and the problems are so complex and vast that I can't possibly have any effect on them, even if I understood them properly, which I don't. We are stuck with the brute reality of human selfishness.

The message of the gospel is that we are each called to play our role in the unfolding of God's plan for creation. Every day, every moment, we either embrace or we reject love, we choose to serve the needs of others or we choose to turn in on ourselves. The future of the world is ours to make.

Lent is a kind of 'exodus', like the exodus journey of the Jewish people from slavery in Egypt to freedom in a new land. It is an invitation to each of us to make a journey with Jesus from the often unjust world in which we live to the new and just one we are destined for.

Brendan Walsh

THE FAVOURABLE TIME

THE CAFOD/CHRISTIAN AID
LENT BOOK 2010

Michael Campbell-Johnston

Ash Wednesday to Saturday After Ash Wednesday

Ash Wednesday

Lent's invitation

Jl 2:12-18; Ps 51; 2 Cor 5:20 – 6:2; Mt 6:1-6, 16:18

> *'Now is the favourable time, this is the day of salvation'.*
> (2 Cor 6:2)

The season of Lent is a privileged time of the year. It offers us the opportunity to stand back from our daily activities and cares, and to ask: 'Where are they all leading?' 'What is the purpose of them all?' Remember Martha and Mary in the Gospel. Mary sat at the feet of Jesus listening to him, whereas Martha was all tied up with the work of running the house and receiving the guests. Jesus said to her: 'Martha, Martha, you worry and fret about so many things, and yet few are needed, indeed only one' (Lk 10:38-42). What is that one thing? Where can I find it? What effect should it have on my daily occupations and cares ?

Jesus also said Mary had chosen the better part. Let us do the same this Lent and try to dedicate some time each day to listening to the Lord. We will need to find a few moments of silence when we won't be interrupted and can escape the noise of people talking all the time, or the radio and television blaring, not to mention mobile phones or other contraptions. But we will also need to seek an inner silence if we are to hear God's voice and this is sometimes harder since our minds are often full of ideas or thoughts chasing themselves around pell mell in our brains. Let us make the effort to let go of them by concentrating on something simple such as our mere breathing in and out.

In the liturgy for Ash Wednesday, St Paul tells us: 'Now is the favourable time, this is the day of salvation.' If we are going to receive the ashes, let them be a symbol that we have heard the Lord's invitation and intend to do our best to accept it. This will mean, as the prophet Joel tells us in the first reading, letting our hearts be broken, not our garments torn. For this is the invitation the Lord is making to each one of us this Lent: 'Come back to me with all your hearts…for (I am) all tenderness and compassion, slow to anger, rich in graciousness, and ready to relent.'

Prayer

Lord, give me your grace and help
to accept your invitation this Lent,
by listening to your voice,
accepting your tenderness and compassion,
and so drawing closer to you.

God's call

Dt 30:15-20; Ps 1; Lk 9:22-25

'When I cry to the Lord, he hears my voice.'

God is calling each one of us this Lent by name, just as God called the prophets in the Old Testament or Jesus called his disciples in the New. And we should reply as they did:

God put Abraham to the test. 'Abraham, Abraham,' God called. 'Here I am,' he replied (Gen 22:1).

God called to him from the middle of the bush. 'Moses, Moses,' God said. 'Here I am,' he answered (Ex 3:1-4).

Yahweh then came and stood by, calling as he had done before, 'Samuel, Samuel.' Samuel answered: 'Speak, Yahweh, your servant is listening' (1 Sam 3: 10).

As Jesus was walking on from there, he saw a man named Matthew sitting by the customs house, and he said to him, 'Follow me.' And he got up and followed him. (Mt 9:9).

But to hear God's call we have to make the effort to listen to God and this is not always easy. We have to seek both outer and inner silence. This is what true prayer is and it is sometimes called 'the prayer of silence'. It means not using words or formulas, or even ideas or imagination, but just being in God's presence. You may remember the wonderful example given by the Curé of Ars who asked an illiterate peasant what he did during the hours he spent on his knees before the Blessed Sacrament. He replied: 'I look at God and God looks at me.'

4

Try and do this in your prayer today because this is the way, as the first reading puts it, 'you will live and increase, and the Lord your God will bless you'. So let us sit at the feet of Jesus, like Mary, and just listen to him. But 'if your heart strays, if you refuse to listen, if you let yourself be drawn into worshipping other gods and serving them, you will most certainly perish ... Choose life, then, so that you and your descendants may live in the love of the Lord your God, obeying his voice, clinging to him, for in this your life consists' (Dt 30:17-20).

Prayer

Lord, I want to hear your call;
help me take the steps needed so that I,
together with many others,
may receive it in our hearts.
Help us all to welcome and follow your voice always.

The Lord's reply

Is 58:1-9; Ps 51; Mt 9:14-15

'The Lord heard me and took pity on me. He came to my help.'

I know the Lord will hear my voice if I cry with a humble and contrite spirit. Today's readings explain what this means. I have to acknowledge my own unworthiness in all its aspects, not just with regard to my own personal sins and private life, but in the effect they have on others and on the world I live in. For they contribute to making the world a worse place, to diminishing the amount of love in it, to destroying the kingdom of love God wants us to build.

This is why God says so clearly in today's reading from Isaiah that the sort of fast that pleases God is:

'to break unjust fetters
and undo the thongs of the yoke,
to let the oppressed go free,
and break every yoke,
to share your bread with the hungry,
and shelter the homeless poor.'

For if you do this, then you will know your light will shine like the dawn.

'Your integrity will go before you
and the glory of the Lord behind you.

Cry, and the Lord will answer;
Call, and he will say, "I am here".'

The lesson could hardly be clearer. If we can put it into
practise and make it a little more real in our lives this Lent,
then the wonderful reply the Lord made through Isaiah
will become more real for us too:

'Do not be afraid, for I have redeemed you;
I have called you by your name, you are mine.
In your old age I shall be still the same,
When your hair is grey I shall still support you.

Does a woman forget her baby at the breast,
Or fail to cherish the son of her womb?
Yet even if these forget,
I will never forget you.' (Is 49:15)

Prayer
Lord, may the humble recognition of my guilt
lead me to struggle for justice
and give myself to the poor and oppressed;
for I know then you will never forget me
or cease to love me.

God is love

Is 58:9-14; Ps 86:1-6; Lk 5:27-32

'Lord, you are good and forgiving, full of love to all who call.'

The Bible gives two definitions of God: philosophical and personal. The philosophical one comes from the Old Testament where God says to Moses: 'I am who am' (Ex 3:14), in other words, perfect self-subsistent being outside time and space. We cannot imagine such a God and would have difficulty in relating to Him/Her. But Jesus became one of us and adopted human nature to bring God nearer to us. The New Testament sees God as Father, Son and Holy Spirit, three persons but one God. And though the Trinity is a mystery we cannot understand, it is one not of isolation or individualism, but of sharing, mutual outpouring, giving and receiving. This is why St John doesn't hesitate to give a second and personal definition: 'God is love.' 'My dear people, let us love one another since love comes from God and everyone who loves is begotten by God and knows God. Anyone who fails to love can never have known God, because God is love' (1 Jn 4:7, 8).

And if God is love, it is no exaggeration to say we are made by love in order to love. In other words, our whole purpose in life is to learn what love is, or better put, to learn how to love. This is why we are in the world, and if we miss out on this, whatever else we might learn, whatever else we might do or achieve, we have missed out on the most important thing of all. This is what Jesus described to Martha as the 'one thing necessary'.

Pope John Paul II described this in a letter to families in very clear words that are well worth pondering: 'Creating the human race in his own image and continually keeping it in being, God inscribed in the humanity of man and woman the vocation, and thus the capacity and responsibility, of love and communion. Love is therefore the fundamental and innate vocation of every human being.' This is true because, as the Catechism puts it, we are 'created in the image and likeness of God who is himself love'.

Prayer

God of love,
help me to understand better
that I and everyone else in the world
are made by love in order to love
and thus share in the love of your own nature.

Michael Campbell-Johnston

First week of Lent

First Sunday of Lent

The temptation of evil

Dt 26:4-10; Ps 91; Ro 10:8-13; Lk 4:1-13

'Be with me, O Lord, in my distress.'

Though God made us in love to share in his own love, we have not always responded to his offer. Each of us has a selfish streak in our nature which puts self first and prevents us from growing in the unselfish love of each other and of God. This is very clearly shown in the temptations Our Lord underwent in the desert at the beginning of his public life and which are related in today's gospel (Lk 4:1-13). They express the three great false hopes of mankind and are as powerful and compelling as ever in our world of today. None of us are free from them so it is important to understand them and see what effect they have on our personal lives, our families and the society we live in.

1. The first temptation, changing stones into bread, is the lure of material wealth and comfort. Today's world offers a dazzling variety of goods and services in our consumerist societies, though restricted to relatively small minorities of the privileged. Yet, as Pope Paul VI argued

in justly famous words: 'Increased possession is not the ultimate goal of nations nor of individuals ... The exclusive pursuit of possessions becomes an obstacle to individual fulfilment and to man's true greatness' (19). The second temptation challenged Jesus to make a show of his power by miraculously saving himself from self-induced injury. Power is sought today by individuals and nations and 'power politics' have become a worldwide phenomenon, backed by the massive sale of destructive weapons by the wealthy to the poor who cannot afford to feed their own citizens. Finally, Jesus was invited to bow down and adore. Modern men and women are similarly tempted to bow down before ideologies, systems of thought or social structures, attributing them absolute rights or claims which end up by enslaving us.

The values of the Kingdom Jesus came to set up are the opposite of these as can be seen clearly in his replies to the tempter, as well as in all his life and teaching. They are the values the world needs for its survival and which each of us should pursue in our own lives.

Prayer
Father, help me to discern the evil
in my own life and in the world around me;
to do all I can to combat it
and so join you in your mission of love and salvation.

The use of things

Lv 19:1-2, 11-18; Ps 19; Mt 25:31-46

'Make yourselves a new heart and a new spirit.'

Both of today's readings emphasize the point that our personal sins or wrongdoing affect not only ourselves but the world we live in. We must not deal fraudulently with our neighbour not bear hatred for him in our heart. On the contrary, 'You must love your neighbour as yourself.' The famous passage in Matthew's gospel describing the last judgement explains why we must do this. 'In so far as you do this to one of the least of these brothers of mine, you do it to me.'

This applies also to our use of things which we can use well, according to God's law, or badly, destroying God's law. Global warming is a good example. It now seems clear beyond any doubt, and agreed by the majority of scientists though some may differ over details, that for the first time in history mankind can and is destroying the world and making it unliveable for future generations. There is increasingly clear evidence, such as freak weather in many parts of the world, that this is beginning to happen already. The amount of carbon dioxide in the atmosphere has already reached its highest level in human history and is nudging ever closer to what is described as a point of no return. The experts agree there is still time for action but it is running out fast.

Pope John Paul II called for an 'ecological conversion'. We have to realize we are meant to be 'stewards of creation' and that the world has been given us to use and develop in accordance with God's plan. We have no right to destroy it now or for future generations. This is not primarily an economic or sociological problem, but a moral one: the difference between what is right and what is wrong. Do I acknowledge this and so recognise that the Pope's call is directed to me as well? If so, am I prepared to do anything about it? Can I accept that a refusal to act, for any reason whatsoever, is a refusal to love my neighbour and therefore to love God?

Prayer

Lord, give me the grace to realise
that I cannot love my neighbour as myself
unless I am concerned with the problem of global
   warming
and prepared to do something about it
in my own personal life and relations with others.

God is concerned

Is 55:10-11; Ps 34; Mt 6:7-15.

'The Lord rescues the just in all their distress.'

When we consider all the injustices and evil in the world, we sometimes feel overwhelmed. We are tempted to say: 'What has all this got to do with me? I am not responsible. I have my job to do, my own life to lead. I should get on with these, and leave the world's problems to those more capable of dealing with them.' Or we may feel: 'Even if I may be partly responsible, I am only one person and the problems are so complex and vast that I can't possibly have any effect on them, even if I understood them properly which I don't. I feel powerless and inadequate.'

Yet we need to realize that we cannot escape being integral parts of the sinful structures in the world. If sin is a rejection of love, an egoistic turning in on self, a denial of God's plan both for me and the universe, then my sin adds to the evil in the world and I cannot separate myself from it. It makes the world a worse place by lowering the amount of true love in the universe and thus helping to destroy attempts to form a civilization built on love. For true love is completely unselfish, a total giving of oneself to the other, like the love of the three Persons in the Holy Trinity.

We therefore need to ask ourselves in all honesty: 'How am I an obstacle to the creative and loving action of God in the world? How am I blocking the work God wants to carry out through me, and thus lessening the value of my own work and even making it counter-productive?' These are not comfortable questions, but today's readings state: 'This poor man called; and the Lord heard him and rescued him from all his distress.' Let us call on the Lord, confident that he will rescue us from all our distress. And let us speak to him in the words of the Lord's prayer that today's gospel tells us Jesus taught his disciples.

Prayer
Our Father in heaven,
may your name be held holy,
your kingdom come,
your will be done,
on earth as in heaven.
Give us today our daily bread,
and forgive us our debts,
as we have forgiven those who are in debt to us.
And do not put us to the test,
but save us from the evil one.

A contrite heart

Jo 3:1-10; Ps 50:3-4,12-13,18-19; Lk 11:29-32

'Come back to me with all your heart, for I am all tenderness and compassion.'

Having recognised and acknowledged our faults, the message of Lent is to turn to God and seek forgiveness. Today's first reading describes how the city of Nineveh repented of its sins and did penance for them. And it says: 'God saw their efforts to renounce their evil behaviour. And God relented: he did not inflict on them the disaster which he had threatened.'

And so it is with us, as the psalm clearly explains. We ask God to blot out our offence, to wash us more and more from our guilt, and to cleanse us from our sin. And we know he will do this for 'a humbled contrite heart, O God, you will not spurn.' In the gospel acclamation God says: 'I take pleasure, not in the death of a wicked man but in the turning back of a wicked man who changes his ways to win life.' And this is because God is 'all tenderness and compassion'.

God forgives immediately and completely without harbouring any grudges or imposing any punishments. His attitude is summed up beautifully in the behaviour of the father in the parable of the prodigal son. Even though the father would have been perfectly justified in imposing some sort of penalty on the son, and even though the son seems to have repented mainly because he was hungry and unhappy in the country where he had gone, the father pays no attention to any of this and not only gives his son an immediate and complete pardon but welcomes him with great joy and happiness. For, as Jesus himself said, 'there will be more rejoicing in heaven over one repentant sinner than over ninety-nine virtuous men who have no need of repentance' (Lk 15:7).

Are we able to forgive in the same way without harbouring grudges or imposing punishments, without looking for revenge? Our world would be so much the better if we and many others could. So let us pray:

Prayer
Father, teach me to forgive,
as you forgave the prodigal son;
teach communities, races and nations
not to bear grudges or look for revenge,
but to treat each other with tenderness and compassion.

Total forgiveness

Est 4:1-3, 5:12-14; Ps 138; Mt 7:7-12

'I thank you for your faithfulness and love.'

Today's gospel explains how full is God's forgiveness, how complete is God's faithfulness and love. Jesus confirms that whatever we ask God in his name, we will receive for 'the one who searches always finds, the one who knocks will always have the door opened to him,' God may not always gives us exactly what we request or in the way we expect it. But this should not diminish our faith for God knows, better than we ourselves, what is really in our best interests. And he adds that, if an earthly father knows how to give his son what is good, 'how much more will your father in heaven give good things to those who ask him'. Queen Esther too realises this and says in her prayer to the Lord: 'Come to my help, for I am alone and have no one but you, Lord.'

So we should rejoice and give thanks to God and can make our own the words of today's responsorial psalm:

'I thank you for your faithfulness and love
Which excel all we ever knew of you.
On the day I called, you answered;
You increased the strength of my soul.

'You stretch out your hand and save me,
Your hand will do all things for me.

Your love, O Lord, is eternal,
Discard not the work of your hands.'

God's love and forgiveness are not for ourselves alone. We are under an obligation to pass them on to others. Today's gospel reminds us: 'Always treat others as you would like them to treat you; that is the meaning of the Law and the Prophets.' Every time we recite the Lord's prayer, we ask God to forgive us as we forgive others. Let us take this opportunity of Lent to examine carefully how we forgive others, whether we forgive them from our hearts.

Prayer
Lord, I thank you for always answering my prayers;
I have complete faith that you always do so,
even if not always in the way I request or expect:
for you in your love know better than I
what is really in my best interest.

A new heart

Ez 18:21-28; Ps 130; Mt 5:20-26

'Make yourself a new heart and a new spirit.'

In today's first reading the prophet Ezekiel uses the word 'integrity' to describe the behaviour of the upright man. If he loses his integrity and renounces it, he copies the wicked man and commits every kind of sin. But if he preserves his integrity and becomes 'law-abiding and honest', then he shall certainly live and shall not die.

Lent is above all a time for conversion. Not conversion in the sense of finding a new faith, but in acknowledging there is something which needs changing in my life. And none of us can claim, if we are honest, that there is nothing that needs to be changed in our life. Lent can help us discover what it is, as well as give us the strength and motivation to take the practical steps needed to remedy it. This can certainly cost us but it is an accurate measure of our love of God in return for his love of us and the forgiveness God has poured out on us. As God says through the prophet Ezekiel: 'I shall pour clean water over you and you will be cleansed; I shall cleanse you of all your defilement and all your idols. I shall give you a new heart and put a new spirit in you; I shall remove the heart of stone from your bodies and give you a heart of flesh instead' (Ezk 36:25, 26).

We must not forget that any true conversion must include a greater concern for the sins of the world. Archbishop Romero of El Salvador put it like this: 'A true

'exodus' we are invited to make with Jesus from the so often unjust world in which we live, into the new and just one we are destined for.

No wonder that Luke calls the mission Jesus left us three times 'The Way'. The first ones who followed Jesus are called in The Acts of the Apostles 'followers of "The Way"' (Acts 9:2). Before Jesus left his disciples, he invited them to travel to the ends of the earth on 'His Way'.

The book of the Acts of the Apostles is one long travelogue of Peter, Paul and so many others. Together they covered practically the whole of the world known to them. And eventually their mission even reached us!

It is good to think in those 'journey' terms during our daily commute to and from work, school and family. The story of the transfiguration is a forecast of the glory that is awaiting us when we follow his way, from the world as it is to the world as it should be.

Thought for the day

Rediscover the real significance of directing your life journey correctly.

Prayer

Lord, help me to walk your path,
joining your journey,
having you intention,
walking Your Way
into the glory to come.

Jesus' empathy

Dan 9:4-10; Ps 79; Lk 6:36-38

'Be compassionate as your Father is compassionate.' (Lk 6: 36)

We can experience sympathy and antipathy for someone. Everyone knows what that means. It is something that often bubbles up in you when dealing with someone. It is also a kind of vibration you sometimes notice yourself when others deal with you. And then there is that other '-pathy': empathy, when you feel and experience a situation in the same way someone else is. It is a situation in which you feel and react as the other, a situation in which you can honestly say, 'I share in your feeling, I share in your life.'

Empathy is openness to the feelings and reality of another. There is an old American Indian Lakota prayer that expresses this kind of relationship: 'Great Spirit, help me never to judge another until I have walked two weeks in his moccasins.'

It is here that that we come very near what compassion means. It is not only being sympathetic, or empathic, it is 'suffering with'. It is opening yourself to the pain and suffering of someone else, the pain and suffering in the world. It is what God did in Jesus Christ.

We are taught that he died to make up for our sins. There is, however, more to his life and his death on the cross than that. He suffered our human lot. He suffered with us the consequences of human error, failure and sin.

He walked in our sandals, one like us, except for sin. As Jon Sobrino, a Jesuit priest and theologian from San Salvador, wrote: 'Jesus identifies with the victims of this world.' He suffered and died on the cross. He was the victim of all that is making so many in our world still victims of human mistakes, offenses, injustices, and even lapses into barbarism.

But he rose from the dead, and his resurrection is 'the foundation of our hope' and at the same time, in the words of Pope Paul VI, an indication of 'our task and mission in this world, "a struggle toward a more humane way of life, that calls for hard work and imposes difficult sacrifices"'(*Populorum Progressio*, 79).

Thought for today
Open your heart, mind and soul to the actual pain and suffering in your world.

Prayer
Compassionate God,
we are engaged in your suffering world,
help us to lead it to a greater justice.
Let us understand this,
see it,
and take it to heart.
Amen.

The Christian challenge in our globalizing world

Is. 1:10, 16-20; Ps 51; Mt 23: 1-12

'...you have only one Father...' (Mt 23: 9)

To hear that our world is getting more and more a global village is not news any more, nor does this information greatly impress us any longer. Practically all of us know that we are interconnected in all kinds of ways – by satellites, telephones, television, radio, e-mail, the internet and in so many other ways. And these are not the only interconnections. The produce we eat and drink, the clothing we are wearing, come from all over the globe. We are increasingly closely related to each other in economic, ecological, social, cultural and other ways.

For many, globalization seems to be a reality we still have to learn to live with. It is in this new context that the reason Jesus gives us to relate to each other might also take on a renewed significance. It is a reason that does not depend on any kind of modern inventions or contemporary developments. It is a reason as old as humankind. It is our common divine origin: '...you have only one Father, and he is in heaven...' (Mt 23:8).

We have one parent, we have one origin, and we belong to the same family. We are all brothers and sisters. Until recently this often seemed to be only talk, but human history proves it to be a fact. We are flying together on the same spaceship, called earth. It might sound like a fairytale, but it is a fact. Have a look at a globe. Get an atlas and have a good look at the world. Get acquainted with the family you have, the world we live in, the spacecraft we are travelling on together. It is the situation Jesus introduced us to when he told a lawyer the story of the good, compassionate Samaritan.

Consider the adventures, the human tragedies, the comedies, the achievements and the failures you were told in your paper, on your radio, in front of your television, or checking your cell-phone today in the family spirit Jesus introduced us to. We are in this all together.

Thought for today
Hold an open place in your heart for all you are dealing with, and practice empathy.

Prayer
Jesus, you prayed:
'That they may be one'
help me to engage myself wholeheartedly in that prayer,
by doing all I can
to overcome all that divides us.
Amen.

On being the greatest

Jer 18:18-20; Ps 31; Mt 23:1-12

> '...the greatest among you must be must be your servant.'
> (Mt 23:11)

The two sons of Zebedee were no heroes, though they dreamed of having the first places in what they thought Jesus' kingdom would be. They wanted to be the winners in the Kingdom they hoped was to come. They wanted to have the greatest possible influence. They were out for the best places. They were career makers, climbing the ladder, hoping to win what we sometimes call the 'rat race'.

All of us know about those dynamics. Even if we ourselves are not inclined or tempted by them, others might nevertheless almost force us into them. A husband might nag his wife for not getting a promotion or a wife might do it to her husband; parents might by pushy with their children. Trying to get higher and higher but never satisfied, or promoted until we exceed our competence, and are never happy again.

The two were no heroes. They came to Jesus with their mother. Did they not dare to ask their question themselves? Did they not dare to take the risk? Answering their mother, but in fact the three of them, Jesus said: 'You do not know what you are asking.' And then turning to the brothers he asked them: 'Can you drink the cup that I am going to drink?' They replied: 'We can.' 'Very well', he said, 'you shall drink my cup'.

The two were not alone. The others were no better.

When they heard what the two had done, trying to climb over their heads, they were indignant. Their anger showed that they had precisely the same ambition. It is Jesus who cuts the whole argument short: 'This is not to happen among you. No; anyone who wants to be great among you must be your servant, and anyone who wants to be first among you must be your slave, just as the Son of man came not to be served but to serve, and to give his life as a ransom for many' (Mt 20:28).

In those few words Jesus offers anyone of us, in whatever position or career we find ourselves, the possibility of making service to others our personal hallmark.

Thought for today
'The only ones among you who will really be happy are those have sought and found how to serve.' (Albert Schweitzer)

Prayer
Jesus, help me to be
the comfort
the support, the joy,
and the service
you want me to be for others.
Amen.

The chasm

Jer 17:5-10; Ps 1; Lk 16: 19-31

> *'...between us and you a great gulf has been fixed...'*
> *(Lk 16:26)*

Jesus' story about the rich man, beautifully dressed and eating and drinking very well, with the poor street person at his front door, is according to those in the know not an original one. Similar stories can be found, so they say, in older ancient literature. No wonder, the story is probably as old as humanity. The poor of the world have been lying and are lying at the gates of the rich all through the ages.

It is the story about a distance between the rich man and the poor beggar. A chasm, that is mirrored in the second part of Jesus' parable. The roles of the two are reversed. That word 'chasm' is the word used in the English translation of Pope John Paul II's encyclical 'The Hundredth Year' (*Centesimus Annus*, 1991) on the social teaching of the Church, which marked the hundredth anniversary of Pope Leo XIII's encyclical 'Of Things New' (*Rerum Novarum*, 1891), the encyclical considered to be the beginning of the Catholic Church's modern social teaching.

According to Matthew's gospel Jesus once said: 'The poor you will always have with you' (26:11). And in the same gospel Jesus told us that whatever we do to the poor, the sick, and those in prison is considered by him as done to himself: 'I was hungry and you gave me food; I was thirsty and you gave me drink; I was a stranger and you made me welcome; naked and you clothed me; sick and you visited me; in prison and you came to see me' (Mt. 25:35-36). He asked us to overcome the chasm not only by charitable works, but by organizing ourselves to bridge the chasm as much as possible.

The conclusions to be drawn from Jesus's parable are hard, when you consider that so many in our world are hungry and helpless. This is even more true and challenging than ever before, as we are better and better informed about the world we inhabit together. No one of us alone can do much to bridge the enormous chasm, but by organizing ourselves and working together, we definitely can.

Thought for today
'Whatever you do to the least one among you is done to me.' (Jesus Christ)

Prayer
Lord,
let me realize
that the world
needs all the power and love,
each one of us
can give.
Amen.

On productivity

Gen 37: 3-4, 12-13, 17-28; Ps 105; Mt 21: 33-43, 45-46

> *'…he sent his servants to the tenants, to collect his produce.'*
> (Mt 21:34)

Every day of the year, in fact almost every hour of the day, news bulletins, news flashes and government information bulletins publish and broadcast statistics and graphs that indicate national production growth or decline, and the values of stocks and shares. This news makes the stock markets bolt and jump. Is there a production increase, or is the economy slowing down? Are we in the red or in the black?

It is news that has a life of its own. Owners and shareholders are often only interested in the profits made by their companies. It is as if nothing else matters as long as production goes up and money is made.

In a way, today's parable suggests that Jesus does the same. He, too, warns those he left behind in the world: 'I tell you, then, that the kingdom of God will be taken from you and given to a people who will produce its fruit' (Mt 21:43). In other words: 'Produce or perish.' Jesus, too, it seems, is exclusively interested in 'production'.

The difference is in what is to be produced. For Jesus, it is God's Kingdom, God's reign among us. Some years ago the National Conference of Bishops in the United States of America described this 'product' in these words:

'We have many partial ways to measure and debate the health of our economy: Gross National Product, per capita income stock market prices, and so forth. The Christian vision of economic life looks beyond them all and asks: Does economic life enhance or threaten our life as a community? With what care, human kindness, and justice do I conduct myself at work? How will my economic decisions to buy, sell, invest, divest, hire or fire serve human dignity and the common good? In what career can I best exercise my talents so as to fill the world with the Spirit of Christ?'

These words lead us during this time of Lent to question our own management of the talents and goods entrusted to us.

Thought for today
Work can be love made tangible.

Prayer
Merciful God,
may life be changed,
so that I may do
more faithfully,
what you expect me to do.
Amen.

Forgive, and be forgiven

Mic 7: 14-15 18-20, Ps 103: 1-4,9-12; Lk 15: 1-3, 11-32

> *'...this son of mine was dead and has come back to life...'*
> (Lk 15: 24)

Someone once told me: 'We are all sinners; the only difference is that some manage to hide it better than others.'

I think this is true. It means that forgiveness, and the gospel story of today, is of interest to all of us. It is of interest for us in three ways. We constantly need to ask for forgiveness, we constantly need to be forgiven, and we constantly need to forgive.

As Martin Luther King put it: 'Forgiveness is not an occasional act; it is a permanent attitude.' Our life is an adventure in forgiveness. No wonder that in the New Testament the word 'forgive' is found 65 times.

To forgive is always a healing process. It is a deliverance. It is the throwing off of a burden by the one who forgives, and by the one who is forgiven. It means for the two parties a liberation, a relief and the regained possibility to be at peace with each other, but also to be at peace with oneself. It is a life-giving release for both parties.

Jesus' parable of the lost or prodigal son is a wonderful example of this gospel truth. The father of the prodigal son explains to his older brother: 'Your brother was dead and has come to life, he was lost and is found' (Lk 15:32). It must have also helped his returning younger son to do what is often the most difficult kind of forgiveness: to forgive oneself. When the prodigal son addressed his father at his return, he tells how he considers himself as lost, not worthy to be called 'your son' any more. In other words, he has written himself off. It is as if he denies in himself the possibility to be any good at all. Jesus' parable describes him as someone who is despicable in his own eyes. He could not think of being forgiven and of forgiving himself. It is the forgiving love of his father that helped him to overcome that blockage in his life.

Thought for today
Forgive, be forgiven and forgive yourself!

Prayer
Lord, have mercy!
Christ have mercy!
Help me
To share in your mercy
Now and forever,
Amen.

Peter Selby

Third Week of Lent

Third Sunday of Lent

The unfairness of life and the justice of God

Ex 3:1-8,13-15; Ps 103; I Cor 10:1-6,10-12; Lk 13:1-9

> *'Unless you repent you all perish as they did.'* (Lk 13:3 and 13:5)

How shall we respond to the unfairness of life? Certainly there's plenty of it around, and hardly a day passes without our reading of the suffering of the innocent. They are the victims of war or crime; they are those overwhelmed by earthquake, fire and flood. And as well as such acute crises and calamities, there are the profound inequalities of life, long term and seemingly embedded in the order of things: the huge burdens of poverty borne by some nations, the inheritance of war and the inequalities faced by individuals with disabilities.

Such are the issues raised in the gospel passage by Jesus' interlocutors, raised of course with no particular intention to engage in a philosophical quest for the truth about the meaning of suffering. Rather the unequal burden of pain and distress is raised as a conundrum, a test to show up some inadequacy in Jesus' teaching ability. He caps their example of the persecuted Galileans with the example of the victims of a calamity in Jerusalem, and with a rhetorical question cuts through any individual connection between someone's sin and their suffering. Were those victims worse sinners than those who were spared? Certainly not.

But the matter does not end there. In this dialogue the questioned becomes the questioner as Christ turns the issue of guilt and responsibility back on those who brought the issue of fairness to him: it was not the Galileans nor the residents of Jerusalem who were shown to be especially evil by the fate they suffered; those who need to ask the question of repentance are those putting the question in the first place. They need to attend to their own status with God if they are not to expect a more severe judgement in the future.

The sight of suffering often leads us to imagine that in some mysterious way it is deserved. Instead it should lead us to a renewed passion for the justice of God to reign supreme in the world. The sight of natural disasters should lead us to renewed efforts to safeguard our planet; the existence of human cruelty and violence should inspire us to create a world that is just and peaceable.

Thought for the day
Which are the instances of human suffering which increase your energy for good; and which are those that make you depressed, or just glad it wasn't you?

Prayer
Lord,
When we see your children suffer
May our compassion be liberated
And our energy for change increased.

Justice – and envy

2 Kings 5:1-15; Ps 42,43; Lk 4:24-30

> ' *of these was cured — only Naaman the Syrian.'* (Lk 4:27)

There's a basic difficulty about the pursuit of justice, as any politician will tell you: in the process of change there are always going to be losers, people who either in reality or in their perception (and that can be just as powerful) will be worse off. The struggles that ensue from any proposed change in the direction of justice will happen as people – that could be any of us – who support justice in principle, and certainly when we feel the victim of injustice discover that for others to be more justly treated may mean they lose out.

Those gathered in the synagogue at Nazareth clearly had no difficulty understanding what Jesus was getting at. Welcoming Jesus' concern for the poor and needy was fine, as long as it did not interfere with their sense of privilege and entitlement. Jesus refers to two stories where God's compassion reached out beyond the boundaries of Israel: Elisha's healing of Naaman the leper (see today's Old Testament reading) and Elijah's visit to the widow of Zarephath (see I Kings 16:8-16). The meaning Jesus drew from those stories – there were many widows/lepers in Israel, but God's care was shown to an outsider – enrages his hearers to the point that they seek to kill him. The story is a rehearsal of what would happen to Jesus in the end as his teaching and compassion reached out, and in the process attacked people's sense of privilege.

Attempts to bring about any change towards justice will always come up against the problem of 'winners and losers' – and it isn't the winners who complain! What that often leads to is the putting of some who see themselves as victims in competition with others, the poor against the poorer, the 'lost sheep of the house of Israel' in competition with the gentiles outside the covenant. Our prayer is for a justice that is genuinely universal; one where if 'win-win' is not possible we manage nonetheless to achieve outcomes that most benefit the most vulnerable. That is our longing – as the psalmist says, 'As the hart longs for flowing streams, so my soul longs for you, O God.'

Thought for the day
How strong is my commitment to justice when I find out what it is going to cost me?

Prayer
Lord,
Make our hearts long for a Justice that flows
Like an ever-flowing stream,
A Justice such as you showed in your Son.

Can restoration be the policy?

Dan 3:25,34-43*; Ps 25; Mt 18:21-35

*Were you not bound to have pity on your fellow-servant just
as I had pity on you? (Mt 18:33)*

The spectacle of bailed-out bankers being begged by the
government to reform their behaviour, to give loans to
help get the economy going and to reduce their bonuses
– and these pleas being ignored – has shocked many, and
angered even more. This financial parable should make
that less shocking. The servant with the large debt is glad
enough to find himself relieved of the burden of a debt he
could not pay. But confronted with a colleague who owes
him a much smaller sum his experience leads him not to
generosity but to caution: he is going to be doubly careful
not to get into serious debt again, and that means hanging
on to his assets. The financial institutions have acted just
like that: bailed out once, they are not going to do
anything that might jeopardise their shareholders'
interests; and the other servants in the parable, no doubt
like the audience who originally heard it, and just like the
general public today, react with outrage.

The parable comes out of an accurate observation of
how people do behave, not how they should. And it is

*Note: the Daniel reference is as it is in the bible as used by
Roman Catholics; those who have the Books of the Apocrypha as
a separate section will find the text in the Prayer of Azaraiah,
verses 2,11-20

told by the one who, having been the bringer of God's mercy to all, predictably receives none himself. And the crowd, outraged by the greed and selfishness of others, turns on him when they learn that mercy is something they not only receive but also are required to show. What Christ offers to the world is not just mercy to those who need it but a whole new policy for the world. We have yet to learn how to work out that policy in terms of our treatment of those who have offended – and because we have not worked that out our prisons are full to overflowing.

That policy, the 'economy' of the Kingdom of God, brings relief from our burdens and forgiveness for our sins. But it is a tough policy, not just a gift. We are invited to surrender the hold we have over others because of their indebtedness to us, just as God has been prepared to show us a mercy we did not deserve.

Thought for the day
If I see someone, as I think, let off too lightly, does it make me angry? Why?

Prayer
Lord,
We pray as you have taught us,
Forgive us our debts
As we forgive those who are indebted to us.

Sustaining freedom demands discipline

Dt 4:1,5-9; Ps 147; Mt 5:17-19

'Do not imagine that I have come to abolish the or the Prophets. I have come not to abolish but to complete them.' (Mt 5:17)

The experience of release is exhilarating, almost intoxicating. Burdens have been lifted; oppressive regimes have been overthrown; vistas of freedom open up like an broad sunny plain after struggling through a dark tunnel. Our television screens have brought us time and again scenes of ecstasy as tyrannies have been overthrown. Yet the maintenance of life in freedom presents challenges to which time and again human beings are unequal. There are, it always turns out, greater difficulties in maintaining order and discipline once freedom has been attained than ever they were while the liberation struggle was going on.

Deuteronomy is cast as Moses' provision for just that situation, for a life in the promised land in which the privations of the slavery they had escaped would quickly be forgotten and the people, and above all their rulers, would lapse into patterns of behaviour that would place their freedom and their very life in jeopardy. It is a book of remarkable wisdom and detail, designed to sustain the memory of what God had done for them and what in turn they must hold on to if their future was to be secure. Rituals to remind the people of how blessed they were sit alongside economic and social requirements designed to regulate their life as the holy people of a holy God.

For the followers of Jesus centuries later there was also a gospel of freedom and the lightening of burdens. But the New Testament abounds with the evidence that the disciplines associated with sustaining gospel freedom were constantly being forgotten and had constantly to be reinforced. In that task the apostles and leaders of the early Christian community were sustained by their fellowship together and by the inspiration of the Holy Spirit. But as today's gospel shows, they had another powerful resource: the memory of the teaching of Jesus who came to bring freedom and yet declared he was not abandoning the law of God's holy people. He untied the burdens of sinners; but the life into which he released them would offer its own challenges and continue to make the demands of the holy life.

Thought for the day
Is this Lent deepening my sense of the challenges of the gospel life?

Prayer
Lord,
We know that to be your slave is to be perfectly free.
Help us to understand and to live the challenge
of this demanding mystery.

Confounding cynicism

Jr 7:23-28; Ps 95; Lk 11:14-23

> *'But some of them said, "It is through Beelzebul, the prince of devils, that he drives devils out."'* (Lk 11.15)

If there is one human tendency that has received a dramatic boost over recent years it is cynicism. The financial world's troubles and the disgracing of significant numbers of Members of Parliament as a result of the expenses scandal have rippled outwards to produce a view of the financial sector and of public life as populated by people who are up to no good – or rather only up to their own good and not there for any social benefit.

That estimate has fed on itself as we have sought and found more and more evidence of wrongdoing and self-interested interpretation of 'the rules'. What has not been asked often enough is the question, 'What do we gain from this feasting on disgrace?' What we lose is clear enough: the financial and business world cannot function without trust, and a situation where those in public life are presumed to be acting only in their own interest produces lower voter turnout and a corresponding lowering of the credibility of anything that politicians do, and therefore the laws they enact: if they can interpret the rules to suit themselves, then so can we all.

The cynical attack on Christ's healing of a possessed person shows that he was not immune from the corrosive effect of cynicism. The suggestion is that his healing powers are manifestations of evil, not of good. He points

46

out that if his healings are manifestations of evil, what about the healings of the many exorcists and healers to whom people in need resorted? Would it not, he asks, be better to see his action as the action of God, a sign of the presence of the Kingdom in the world?

And might it not be better, we might ask, to continue to see the professions that channel investment and the work of politics as spheres of vocation, signs that God touches individuals to seek the good of their fellow human beings? There'd still be wrongdoing, and we'd still have to search it out; but we would not allow that to corrupt our capacity to seek the good and recognise it when it is there.

Thought for the day
Do I share the popular interest in the wrongdoing of others?

Prayer
Lord, even your Son was said to be up to no good.
Be present with all those who are in any disgrace.
Turn their hearts, and the hearts of all,
to recognise goodness wherever it appears,
and to rejoice in it.

True religion

Hos 14:2-10; Ps 81, Mk 12:28-34

'You are not far from the Kingdom of God.' (Mk 12:34)

A survey comparing the leading members of a church with members of society in general led one sociologist to declare the religious on the whole grumpier. This is not a flattering description, but fairly accurately points to a tendency believers share to discover what is wrong with the world, in which ways it is getting worse – and of course all the ways in which it used to be better! The criticisms are often spot on; but there's a sense that to discover something good and celebrate it would show a lack of prophetic zeal, and a corresponding energy to find things to complain about.

Jesus has left us, by contrast, a legacy of teaching that is remarkable for his pointing to the good he found in unlikely places, and confronting those who were sure they were his followers and knew how to be aware of the wickedness in the world around them with the goodness residing in those whom they disliked or condemned. The parables are full of unlikely characters who have lessons to teach the righteous, drawn often from the world of commerce. Jesus had no hesitation in pointing to the difficulty facing the rich in entering the kingdom of heaven – and also no hesitation in pointing out that dishonest stewards and hard businessmen had lessons to teach those who were on the way to the kingdom.

They needed to know that there were scribes and

lawyers to be celebrated also, like this one who among all the commandments in the Law knew what really mattered. He was not far, said Jesus, from the Kingdom. He represents a call to us all to be prepared for surprises when it comes to the search for goodness and to be prepared to celebrate it when we do.

The stereotypes with which we often operate prevent us from being surprised and delighted by goodness. Snobbery, including inverted snobbery, negative views about 'young people' or 'old people', constantly get in the way of our discovering God and closeness to God; and in doing so they may prevent us from looking again at our estimate of ourselves.

Thought for the day
Am I open to being surprised by goodness – today?

Prayer
Lord God,
you surprise us constantly with the signs of your presence
and your working in the lives of your children.
Give us hearts open to find you among us,
And the love of you where we had not looked.

Whom does God welcome?

Hos 5:15-6:6; Ps 51; Lk 18:9-14

'Everyone who raises himself up be humbled, but anyone who humbles himself be raised up.' (Lk 18:14)

Being grateful for not having to be in the situation of others is not unusual. When we choose where to live, find schools for our children, join our clubs, choose with whom to spend our time – in short when we express our priorities not by words but by our actions – we constantly make choices that show the situation we want to be in – and the situations we are grateful to be able to avoid. In making those choices we may simply be cautious – not living in areas prone to flooding, for instance. But in making those choices we may also display in unmistakeable ways the view we imagine God takes of people.

And there we may just be wrong. The Pharisee had much to be thankful for, in having a life pattern which accorded with the Law. And he notices that he has not become subject to the constraints and the contempt of a person branded as a sinner. But that thankfulness that seemed so reasonable suffered from one flaw that he had not recognised: what presented itself to him as thankfulness to God was in reality a form of self-exaltation; and in that process the reality of God's love was being consistently misunderstood.

In all his teaching and ministry Jesus never asks people to abandon the righteousness in which they had been formed, the righteousness of the Jewish law. What his miracles, his parables – and the company he chose – reveal is a divine love that seeks those whom human beings do not seek to be with. The problem about us when we 'raise ourselves' is that we are in the process putting down not just our fellow human beings but the God who loves all, especially those who are unloved.

There is much that we do not know about God's kingdom and what it might be like. But two things we can be sure of: first, it is a realm where we shall not be permitted to choose the other members; and secondly we shall be delighted by all whom God has chosen.

Thought for the day
If the sinner was more justified than the Pharisee, where does that leave me?

Prayer
God of mercy and grace,
your Son avoided nobody in his seeking of the lost.
May we see in the world's outcasts
the children whom you especially love.

Katherine Schexneider

Fourth Week of Lent

Fourth Sunday of Lent

Forgiveness

Jos 5: 9-12; Ps 35; 2 Cor 5: 17-21; Lk 15: 1-3, 11-32

> *'While he was still a long way off, his father caught sight of him, and was filled with compassion.'* (Luke 15.20)

In the psalm set for today, we hear the well-familiar theme of the man obsessed with his enemies. The speaker bemoans them, curses them, and implores God to destroy them. We can imagine this man's anxiety. It's all consuming. Forgiveness? No way. 'Brandish lance and battle-axe against my pursuers' (Ps 35: 3a).

Luke's gospel reading turns this approach on its head. The father not only forgives his wayward son, but does so unilaterally, even before the son gives his 'I've really goofed up' speech. In an instant, all is forgiven. The father is analogous to God, the God who forgives in the blink of an eye. It's the sulky brother whom we can compare to the narrator in the psalm. Neither can get beyond his hostility; neither can forgive. In the Old Testament, we might see his anger as righteous, might expect God to crush the man's enemy. That won't happen in the gospel. God as the parable father wants to hear nothing about his son's resentment. 'Get over it. Move on. It's time to celebrate.' This theology is really different. This is good news.

As prodigal sons and daughters ourselves, we find great comfort in the forgiveness by the father. But the behaviour of the brother speaks to us as well. We are called to let go of our resentments, get out of our own way and forgive—forgive our sibling, our co-worker, our neighbour. So there is good news here not only for the prodigal son, but also for his brother who is invited to let go of his anger. We're not sure if he received it, though. We don't know how the story turned out for him. He may have gone off and read Psalm 35 and commiserated with its narrator. How will the story turn out for us? Will we get the good news? As we carry around resentments against a family member or boss or co-worker like a ball and chain on our ankle, we can see that we too are invited to let go, to forgive in an instant, to open wide the door to our heart, and to let the feast begin.

Thought for the day
Whom can I forgive this Lenten period?

Prayer
O God, who gives us the gift of forgiveness,
Help me to let go of the anger
I hold against those close to me.
Unshackle me from the chains of resentment,
That keep me away from others,
And from you.

New creation...today!

Is 65: 17-21; Ps 30; Jn 4: 43-54

'Lo, I am about to create new heavens and a new earth.' (Is 65:17a)

While I spent a year in Afghanistan working with local physicians, I had the wonderful opportunity to participate in a community aid project at a primary school in Kabul. We distributed school supplies to the dozens of children who did their best to learn in a building with no heat or electricity and only a few broken benches instead of proper desks. And no pencils, notebooks or paper.

Hundreds of people throughout my country generously provided the supplies we handed out. These everyday folks would never enjoy that beautiful moment of personally handing out a superhero backpack to a small boy, but purchased and shipped the backpacks anyway. These anonymous benefactors engaged in a creative gesture, reached out across the world, and made a small but meaningful inroad into poverty. Now, more Afghan children have the tools to learn, and with better education, the tools to improve their country in their own creative way.

In Isaiah, we hear of God's plan to create a new Jerusalem, a better one, full of hope. Isaiah reminds us that God creates continually in our world. We often think of divine creation as Genesis 1, but the divine hand did not stop there. It continues throughout the Old and New Testaments, and to our own day. Isaiah also reminds us of our own responsibility in the building process. In verse 21, he speaks of the literal building of houses and the planting of vineyards as integral parts of the new city. The ancient Israelites were summoned to be co-creators, side by side with their God.

We, too, are called to the workbench of new creation. We, too, must share in the work to make 'Jerusalem a joy.' We, too, can contribute to a world of 'rejoicing and happiness.'

This Lent, let us look for fresh opportunities to share with God in the joyous labour of creation until 'no longer shall the sound of weeping be heard,' wherever there still exists poverty or hunger or pain.

Thought for the day
Where is God's creative hand at work in my community, and how can I join my hand with his?

Prayer
God, you are the Creator
Who continually shapes our world.
Help us find ways to share in your efforts.
Help us turn suffering into joy.

Stealth contributions

Ezek 47: 1-9, 12; Ps 46; Jn 5: 1-3, 5-16

'The man who was healed did not know who it was, for Jesus had slipped away.' (Jn 5: 13)

'Let's all give the Altar Guild volunteers a round of applause for their work this Advent Season.' On cue, applause does indeed ripple from the pews as the members of the Altar Guild beam and graciously accept the praise from the congregation. They would do this work anyway, because they are dedicated, but it feels wonderful to bask in the limelight even if just for a few moments. It is a natural human emotion to desire recognition and appreciation for one's labours. Jesus, though fully human, was so different.

In today's gospel story about healing on the Sabbath, we hear yet another example of Jesus doing some amazing act, and then dodging quickly from any impending limelight. We might argue that he feared retribution, from the Jews or authorities, but I find that an inadequate response. He didn't fear the consequences of his actions. He faced them, even unto death.

Jesus shunned the adoration and celebrity status he might have gained (and did gain). Perhaps the best explanation is humility. For all of his power, to heal and forgive, he was the humblest of men. He preached this message and lived it to the same degree. He also understood that his Father would ultimately judge his life's work, and not just the way his life ended, but the whole body of work. Can we try to imitate that approach?

Can we detach ourselves from the plaudits of others? Can we just roll up our sleeves and do the job set out for us and then quietly slip away? Can we loosen our grasp on the praise we expect from our family and friends and co-workers, let it slip through our fingers and settle on the workbench whilst we move on to the next event without a fuss? Can we accept as wholly sufficient the knowledge that God sees our efforts and is pleased by them?

This Lent, let us take a moment in the morning to commit to practicing stealth contributions and another moment in the evening to sit in silence bundled up in God's warm comforter of gratitude.

Thought for the day
Today, I'll stay in the background.

Prayer
O God, remind me that your love and acceptance
Are enough in this world.
For they are.

Come out of the darkness...and into my neighbourhood

Is 49: 8-15; Ps 145; Jn 5: 17-30

'Saying to the prisoners: Come out!'

The headscarf. It made her stand out in the grocer's, made her seem even more different than the native English in my town, as if her inability to speak English and the fact that she kept to herself wasn't enough. She and her husband had moved into the neighbourhood a few months ago, with their three small children and a woman who was probably a sister or cousin. He worked at a restaurant that served Afghan food; she stayed home and managed the children.

I hadn't ever tried to speak to her. We spoke different languages, of course, but I also hesitated because I didn't understand Afghan or Muslim culture and was afraid I'd say something wrong and offend her. And frankly, I wasn't sure what we could talk about anyway. They came from a place of darkness, not unlike what Isaiah describes in the reading for today. How could I connect with someone from such a different background?

That day in the grocer's, something changed. She had made a large purchase and at the counter she was struggling with her bags and trying to keep her kids in tow. I'm sure she didn't know how to ask for help and was probably too shy to ask anyway. On an impulse, I approached her and offered to carry some of her parcels, using a combination of words and hand gestures. To my surprise, she smiled and motioned down the street toward her flat. I followed and, thinking I had nothing to lose, made a few pleasant comments (in English, of course). She would stare at me, then answer enthusiastically (in Dari, of course), becoming more engaging and animated as we walked.

At her flat, I politely said goodbye, while she thanked me (this much I could figure out) profusely. A warm smile was translation enough, though. And there on the porch, she ceased to be an anonymous Muslim woman seemingly covered in clothes and scarves and this funny culture I didn't understand. She became Ramzia.

And there was light.

Thought for the day
Who is my neighbour?

Prayer
O God, when prisoners of poverty and war and oppression
Come to share my homeland,
Let me welcome them into the light.
Let me reach out to them,
As you do to us,
With open arms.

Toe-to-toe with God

Ex 32: 7-14; Ps 106; Jn 5: 17-30

> *'So the Lord relented in the punishment he had threatened to inflict on his people.'* (Ex 32: 14)

Does God change his mind? In the story of the golden calf, the Israelites are anxious about Moses' return from the mountain, where he is receiving the tablets containing the Ten Commandments. Aaron takes golden earrings from the women and fashions them into a molten calf, which the Israelites then worship as a symbol of the Lord. This act somehow comforts them in Moses' absence. By making an image of the Lord, though, they incur God's wrath, and he tells Moses that he will consume them in a blaze.

Moses doesn't passively accept this threat. He stands toe-to-toe with God, reminding him of his relationship with Abraham, Isaac and Jacob, that their descendants are to be as many as the stars in the sky. He throws in the word 'promise' in my edition (The New American Bible) for good measure. Moses challenges God to remain true to his word, to stay engaged in the sometimes-bumpy relationship with the people of Israel. What was he thinking!

The story continues with Moses confronting Aaron for his bad idea, and another episode of Moses and the Lord negotiating atonement. But we might just stop here, at the end of today's passage, and ask what it means to have Moses hashing it out with God and God changing his mind about punishing the Israelites. Does God change his mind? Can we change God's mind with our pleas?

What would it look like if we had the opportunity to approach God, up close as Moses did, and to ask him to do one thing for us, for our community, for our world? What speech would we prepare as we walked up the mountain? How we would start the conversation? How would we account for our own actions, our own part in the troubles of the world? What would we ask God to change? What would it be like if we really stood that close to God? Would it be different from our daily prayer as we practice it now? How?

Take a few minutes today to indulge in some creative imagery about standing toe-to-toe with God. He might just be listening.

Thought for the day
If he listened to Moses, why not me?

Prayer
O God, now I will stand before you
blameless and unafraid.
I will tell you what I think,
and I will ask you to change course.

Heaven on earth

Wis 2: 1, 12-22; Ps 34; Jn 7: 1-2, 10, 25-30

> *'Brief and troublous is our lifetime.'* (Wis 2: 1b)

'Life's too short for ....'

'She is free from the pains of this life now and is in a better place.'

'God took him from us too young.'

'Work sucks but I need the bucks.' (car bumper sticker)

Well, which is it then? Are our lives too short or too long? Is life on this earth a painful penance to be endured or a source of invigoration? Like the people in the passage from Wisdom, who, in the writer's opinion, were 'not aright' in their outlook, we struggle to make sense of our lives on earth. What can we hang onto?

Well, Heaven of course. The next life. Paradise. We will reunite with all the souls of the departed, meet Jesus in person. The agonies of this life will slip away with our final breath, and we'll have peace and joy like we've never known. So just hold on. It will get better. And, as Christians, we believe that Jesus open the gates for us in a unique way.

Certainly, Jesus alludes to Heaven, and, in the reading today, he makes one of many references to his Father sending him to spend a human life on earth (Jn 7: 29). And in our education as Christians, we develop a strong sense of what heaven might be like. Wonderful!

But Jesus was far more focused on a Kingdom of Heaven right here and right now, in his own time and in ours. His parables give us the blueprint for conducting our affairs and relationships. If the author of Wisdom could say that those depressing folks had gotten it wrong, then Jesus gives us the solution – here's how to make this world a prelude to the next. Here's how bring the love of God to your neighbour, whomever he is and for the duration of your life, long or short.

Do we fall into the trap of the characters of Wisdom and find our own lives burdensome? Is our thinking not aright? Are we just holding out for the next life? Or do we follow Jesus right here and right now to bring a little paradise into our homes, our workplaces, our communities?

Thought for the day

How can I make someone's life a little less troublous today?

Prayer

O God, help me not to lose faith in this world.
Let me bring your Kingdom to others
in some small way
right here and right now.

Where are you from?

Jer 11: 18-20; Ps 7; Jn 7: 40-52

'The Messiah will not come from Galilee, will he?'
(Jn 7:41b)

'Hey, where are you from anyway?' Nassir had come to expect this question as the new kid in the neighborhood, and because his dark skin and black hair suggested he was from southwest Asia. The boys didn't threaten him, but they weren't too friendly either.

'I'm from Kabul, Afghanistan,' he answered.

'Where's your kite?' one of them snickered.

Nassir remained silent for a moment, then walked away.

'OK, we've got to pick the house representative for the cross country race next week. Let's hear your choices.'

'Perkins …. McAllister.'

'What about Nassir?' one of them offered. The other boys looked around uncomfortably.

'He's the fastest. You've seen him run. I mean, we are trying to win, right?'

'Of course, we are. I'm just not sure if he's the one we want in such an important race,' Jones, the house captain, countered. He stared out the window for a minute, drumming his fingers on the sill, eyeing the school chapel in the distance. In his mind's eye, he could see Nassir gliding through the wooded course with his easy form. Still, one didn't know what he was made of, did one? He turned around.

'Perkins.'

His G.P. had broken the news: he had leukemia. It was one of the more treatable forms, but it was terrifying nonetheless. Now he sat in the referral clinic, waiting to meet the oncologist who would treat him. His G.P. had told him this doctor was excellent, one of the best.

'Hi. I'm Dr. Nassir Khan. Come on into my office Mr Jones.'

Jones immediately recognized him, that same muscular frame and graceful walk.

'I, I remember you from school,' he stammered. 'I was house captain.'

'Oh, yes, I do remember you. Yes. Well, let's talk about your leukemia and how we can help you.' His voice and manner betrayed no resentment, no vindictiveness. Jones scanned the wall and saw pictures of a university running team and Nassir flying a kite with his son. He felt so tired. The leukemia was sapping his strength. He couldn't hold Nassir at arm's length any longer.

'Please help me.'

'I will, Jones, I will.'

Thought for the day
In whom will I find Christ today?

Prayer
Jesus, let me see your face in people from every land.
Deliver me from judging others
On the basis of where they're from.
Let me welcome them all to the table
As you did.

Clare Amos

Fifth Week of Lent

Fifth Sunday of Lent

The dawning of God's new day

Is 43: 16-21; Ps 126; Ph 3: 8-14; Jn 8: 1-11

'He bent down and wrote on the ground.' (Jn 8: 6)'

During each of the next five days, the Gospel reading comes from John 8. Underlying this chapter of the Gospel is the symbol of light. The theme carries on into the following chapter (9) and what we read through discussion and argument in chapter 8, is then graphically illustrated through action – the story of giving sight to a man born blind. Both chapters 8 and 9 reflect what it means for Jesus to claim, 'I am the light of the world' (John 8.12; 9.5).

So the tripartite encounter between Jesus, a woman charged with adultery and her accusers (John 8.1-11), is the opening sally in this chapter which eventually becomes both a powerful and a painful contest between light and darkness. Appropriately this first incident takes place 'Early in the morning', at the time when the light begins to shine – and on the Mount of Olives. This mountain towers above Jerusalem to the east, and just as the coming of day was heralded by the sun appearing over its crest, so also Old Testament traditions spoke of the Mount of Olives as the place where God would suddenly appear to come and judge his people (Zechariah 14.4).

In Jesus' deliberations and action in relation to the woman in her apparently hopeless situation, we see the light beginning to shine. It does not yet reach the powerful – even harsh – noonday glow that we will experience later in this chapter. Rather it warms us gently as Jesus allows and encourages us – and the protagonists in the story – to make their own decisions and shape their own future. As Rowan Williams has commented in *Writing in the Dust*, the small book he penned after his own experience in New York close to Ground Zero on 11 September 2001, what is notable is that Jesus stops, does not speak hastily, but rather simply writes in the dust of the ground. And so he 'allows a moment, a longish moment, in which people are given time to see themselves differently precisely because he refuses to make the sense they want. When he lifts his head, there is both judgement and release.' Then in eventually using the word 'sin' to both the crowd and to the woman he invites all to 'give up old ways and enter a new way of life' (Gail O' Day).

Thought for the day
What issues and concerns are there in our day over which we need to 'write in the dust' rather than rush to judgement?

Prayer
Lord who looked,
Glance upon us even today.
We fear your eyes,
For they offer us both judgement and compassion.
Give us the strength to meet your gaze
and the confidence to look with you for what needs to be transformed in our world today.

The crisis of light and love

Dan 13: 1-9, 15-17, 19-30; Ps 23; Jn 8:12-20

'I judge no one.' (Jn 8.15)

Part of the richness of John 8 is that (along with chapters 7 and 9) it reflects on the themes of the Feast of Tabernacles, a major pilgrimage feast celebrated by the Jewish community each year in September or October. The feast recalled the years that the people of Israel had spent wandering in the wilderness – with God present and guiding them through the pillar of flame. To help people to remember this, at the celebration of Tabernacles each year great torches were lit on the Temple platform. The light from them could be seen throughout all Jerusalem. So when Jesus speaks of himself as 'I am the light of the world'(8.12), he is deliberately recalling – yet also challenging – this custom.

Now it is no longer those static lights confined within a holy place whose glow will extend through all the world, but this human being, God's Word made flesh, who will be the means through which we may see God present: 'the glory of God shining in the face of Christ Jesus' (2 Cor 4.6).

The St John's Bible, a modern illuminated Bible produced by the Benedictine Abbey of Collegeville, Minnesota, has many stunning illustrations, including one of the Word in process of becoming flesh. The illustration encourages us to reflect on the way that the light of Christ, gradually, perhaps even painfully, takes shape to imprint itself on the darkness of the world into which it comes.

Light is a powerful symbol for the divine. It is not surprising that it recurs throughout many religions. In the Gospel of John Jesus' role as 'Light of the World' is linked closely to the theme of 'judgement'. Yet John gives this motif a powerful twist. 'I judge no one' (8.15), says Jesus. He does not have to, for people judge themselves by their response to the light – whether they choose to draw near or whether they seek to scurry away and hide, unable to bear the truths that the light will reveal to them and about them. The choice is theirs. And yet of course if the light had not come, this 'crisis' of choice would not have arisen (our word 'crisis' is linked to the Greek verb *krino* = judge) and we could have continued to wallow comfortably in the gloom.

Prayer for the day
Do we like Jesus' first listeners, find it difficult to forgive him for forcing us to make choices that we would prefer to avoid?

Prayer
Radiant Lord of glory
Source of light and life,
You shine your penetrating rays
Throughout all creation,
And catch us in your glow
Refusing to let us hide from your love.
May we learn to reflect your generosity,
Offering a lamp of hope to our neighbours
As we climb hand in hand with them on the journey
Towards the city set on a hill,
the glorious city of God
where your welcoming grace is made visible to all.

The meeting-point between earth and heaven

Num 21: 4-9; Ps 102; Jn 8: 21-30

> *'When you have lifted up the Son of Man, then you will realise that I am.'* (John 8. 21-30)

It was at the Exodus and during Israel's time in the wilderness, the epoch which was commemorated by the Feast of Tabernacles, that God had revealed his name to his people: 'I am who I am' (see Exodus 3.14 and 34.6). When, in John's Gospel, Jesus proclaims 'I am', he is deliberately recalling and reclaiming for himself the divine name. Most of us are probably aware of the 'obvious' 'I am' statements, such as 'I am the bread of life' (6.35) or, as earlier in this chapter, 'I am the light of the world' (8.12). But there are also a number of 'I am' statements in John which are half hidden by English translations, but which in Greek use the same words *ego eimi* – 'I am'. There are four of these in John 8. In today's passage they appear in verse 24 ('You will die in your sins unless you believe that I am') and verse 28 ('When you have lifted up the Son of Man, then you will realise that I am'). They add to the rich texture of John's understanding of Jesus that he wants to share with us. For the phrase links together humanity and divinity. When he uses these words Jesus is affirming his real humanity – he is a person who is really present with his friends (and adversaries) in their lives in first century Palestine. It is no accident that many 'I am' statements are linked to basic aspects of human existence (Bread, Light, Life, Gate, Vine). At the same time however his claim 'I am' opens a doorway to the divine – to the God who had been worshipped since the beginning of time and history. And Jesus' use of the phrase in this way suggests that humanity and divinity are not (potentially at least) opposites that are poles apart: rather that it is by coming to a more profound understanding of what humanity and life in its fullness can be that we shall be able to experience the divine. So in verse 28 Jesus links this claim 'I am' to his 'lifting up' on the cross. The cross is the bridge between earth and heaven, the place which has allowed the realms of 'below' and 'above' to meet forever more. Jesus' willing embrace of the cross is not a negation of his humanity – or his divinity – but has allowed the doorway to God opened by his human life to remain open for ever and for all.

Prayer for the day
Is it true, in your experience, that we can glimpse God more clearly through coming to cherish the potential fullness of human life?

Prayer
Jesus, Son of God,
Bridge between earth and heaven,
For our sake you emptied yourself,
Revealing your glory and
gifting us life.
May we who have glimpsed such generosity,
Respond with full and thankful hearts,
Reflecting and sharing your profligate love,
which refuses to be satisfied
until it has transfigured the whole world.

Challenged by the truth

Dan 3: 14-20, 24-28, 52-56; Jn 8: 31-42

'The truth shall set you free.' (John 8.31-42)

This passage – and the one chosen by the lectionary for tomorrow (John 8.51-59) – are interesting not only for what they say but also for the verses between them which the lectionary editors have chosen to leave out. Their decision was hardly surprising, for John 8. 43-50 is one of the most difficult passages in the entire New Testament. The language that John places on Jesus' lips in these verses as he confronts his opponents becomes viciously hostile, and may bear considerable responsibility for the long history of Christian anti-semitism. For example, the description of the Jews as children of the devil (8.44) was repeated in a picture book for children published by the Nazi government in 1936. Even in the verses that do fall within today's passage the temperature of the exchange has already become heated.

It is however interesting to realise that these apparently harsh words are addressed to 'the Jews that had believed in him' (8.31). They are not a critique of people who had been hostile to Jesus from the start, but rather are spoken to men and women who had been, at least for a time, his supporters. And the dialogue opens not with a rebuke, but with an invitation – to 'remain' or 'abide' in Jesus' word – and a promise, that they would come to know the truth which would set them free. That phrase 'the truth will make you free' is the motto of the worldwide Anglican Communion, and so particularly dear to me. Reflecting on the kind of truth that sets people free, I am reminded that all too often we think of truth as a possession – our possession – that we can so easily use as a weapon with which to batter others. That is not the kind of truth that sets either us, or those others, free. One of the crucial insights of John's Gospel is that 'truth' is not a static object. Rather it is an invitation to participate in an ongoing journey with Jesus, living ever more deeply and closely alongside him and allowing him to be our guide. So, for example, 'truth' is linked in John 14.6 to the word 'way' and in Jesus' farewell words we learn that the 'Spirit of truth', the means by which Jesus will remain with his followers, will continually lead them into a deeper and fuller understanding of this reality. Indeed it may be those who refuse to accompany Jesus on this exhilarating journey who will discover, like those addressed in John 8.31, that they have 'lost' the truth, for Jesus himself has travelled on ahead.

Thought for the day

What are the things from which we need to be 'set free' and how can the truth that Jesus offers us enable us to accept such an offer of freedom?

Prayer

Come, my Way, my Truth, my Life:
such a way as gives us breath,
such a truth as ends all strife,
such a life as killeth death.

(George Herbert)

God's freedom to be God

Gen 17: 3-9; Ps 105; Jn 8: 51-59

'Before Abraham was, I am.' (Jn 8.58)

These verses form a stunning climax to John chapter 8. In them the light blazes out in a way that compels and challenges our gaze. They may offer at least a partial solution to the hostility that has built up throughout the discussion between Jesus and his questioners; they certainly offer an immense challenge to the Church through all time. In my reflection on Tuesday I commented on the repeated 'I am' on the lips of Jesus – and now the discussion dramatically concludes with his claim, 'Before Abraham was, I am' (8.38).

In breaking through all the rules of Greek tenses in this way, Jesus is asserting his eternal identity with God. Yet this apparently absolute claim may open up wider horizons for all people of faith – Christians included. For when God first claimed the name of 'I am', according to Exodus 3.14, both context and language suggest that at least part of its significance is God's refusal to be held captive by the 'boxes' in which human beings all too often seek to control the divine. And so the name 'I am who I am' is God's assertion of God's sovereign freedom and uncontrollability – a freedom that can stand in judgement on our systems, even our religious systems, however well intentioned they may be.

Is there not here a plea for us all to be more than we imagine ourselves to be, beyond the constraints of our tradition and identity? Can we say that his claim 'I am' critiques our own cherished religious traditions and institutions – perhaps even how we use the Bible? The great biblical scholar Raymond Brown puts it like this: 'Sooner or later Christian believers must wrestle with the limitations imposed on the Scriptures by the circumstances in which they were written.'

Yet Jesus' assertion, 'Before Abraham was, I am' are words of welcome as well as of judgement. The theme of light that has run through this chapter links us back to creation, and God's willingness to shine on all. And in embracing Abraham, and the Samaritans (8.48), and in asserting an origin before both, Jesus includes, potentially, all who are willing to abide in him.

Thought for the day

What challenges does it offer for you to reflect on Jesus as 'I am who I am'?

Prayer

Jesus, mysterious 'I am',
Word proceeding from the Father,
underwriting all creation,
stretch our hearts and grant us a generous vision of God's mission,
Enabling all to share in the graciousness of the Holy Trinity.

Holy place and gateway to God

Jer 20: 10-13; Ps 18; Jn 10: 31-42

'The one whom the Father has consecrated.' (Jn 10: 31-42)

Stones, and the threat of stoning, seem to feature prominently in this week's Gospel readings. There was the woman who Jesus protected from the threat of stoning by his gracious silence; there was the near stoning that Jesus experienced at 8.58 – averted by his hiding and leaving the temple; and now – back once again the Temple – the threat to Jesus recurs.

Stones and Jerusalem somehow seem to belong together. In the New Testament at one point Jesus speaks of the city's stones crying aloud in welcome to their Messiah (Luke 19.40) and yet only a few verses later mourns the destruction of the city in which not one stone will be left upon another (Luke 19.44).

Having been privileged to live for five years in Jerusalem I can witness to the heart-stopping physical beauty of the city – connected somehow with its stones, out of which its buildings are constructed. As Gerald Butt's prayer, part of which is quoted below, puts it, they play a duet with the phases of the strong sun and the region's clarity of light. Yet Jerusalem's beauty is also its tragedy. An ancient Jewish proverb sums it up:'Ten parts of beauty gave God to the world, nine to Jerusalem and one to the reminder; ten parts of sorrow gave God to the world, nine to Jerusalem and one to the reminder.'

Love for Jerusalem can turn swiftly to desire for possession and then on to hatred and strife. At the heart of Jerusalem in New Testament times was the Temple. A magnificent building, it was venerated as the dwelling of God, and the place God where could be accessible to human beings. And so, like the city itself, it became the object of control by the priestly class, who thus found themselves able to have power over who would have access to God, and on what terms. Today's Gospel reading is set during the Feast of Dedication or Hanukkah (10.22), a festival that commemorated the re-consecration of the Temple during the time of the Maccabees after a period of defilement. In 10.36 Jesus deliberately chooses to use the word 'consecrated' (translated 'sanctified' in NRSV) of himself. In claiming for himself a word that contemporary religious tradition used for the Temple building, he is asserting that now it is through his incarnate body rather than the stones of a Temple building that human beings can draw near to God. Access is no longer to be controlled by a priestly caste, and is open to all (such as the blind man in John 9) who because of race, or disability or gender would previously have been kept at a distance.

Thought for the day
What are the ways in which we try to possess and control access to God?

Prayer
O Lord soften the stone hearts
of those who preach and practise
intolerance and bigotry;
as the sun's setting glow
softens the stone walls
of your Holy City, Jerusalem.
(Gerald Butt)

The fulcrum of our faith

Ezek 37: 21-28; Jer 31: 10-13; Jn 11: 45-56

'To gather into one the dispersed children of God.'
(Jn 11.45-56)

These verses are the turning-point around which John's Gospel revolves, chronologically and theologically. They are also, for Christians, the turning-point of history. Immediately before this Jesus has raised Lazarus from the dead; now, as a direct result of his actions, his own death is being plotted. Jesus' giving of life to another will imminently lead to his own death. It is a vivid narrative demonstration of our theology of the cross, 'He died that we might live'. And so these verses act as a bridge between the 'signs' that have dominated the first eleven chapters of the Gospel, and Jesus' passion, whose swift approach is made clear in the incident which immediately follows as Mary anoints Jesus 'for his burial' (12.1-8).

In the Gospel of John the characters in the story sometimes speak more than they know. It is a mark of the Gospel writer's sense of irony and paradox. So it is here.

First, the priests and Pharisees complain about the many signs that Jesus has performed – signs which, as we can see, have systematically shown that Jesus has come to bring life in all its fullness (John 10.10). Paradoxically, for these religious leaders, such signs are fearful. Their fear is focused around the possible 'death' of the 'holy place', the Temple, whose relevance and integrity has been systematically challenged by Jesus in the Gospel's preceding chapters.

78

And then with savage irony the Gospel writer places upon the lips of Caiaphas the high priest a stunning example of the politics of expediency: 'It is better to have one man die for the people, than to have the whole people destroyed.' The essential task of the high priest was to seek to atone for the nation (Exodus 30.10), to focus in himself the priestly task of suffering on behalf of the people of God – if necessary, even to die in order that others might live. Yet with his words of real politik Caiaphas speaks more than he knew and unwittingly bequeaths this high priestly role to Jesus. This is a role that Jesus so clearly accepts in the High Priestly prayer of John 17, and as sacrificial victim in the events of the following day. Yet in accepting in his own body these roles of temple and priest Jesus transforms them. They are no longer confined by time or space, no longer restricted by the limitations of race or nation; their benefits are now available to all the 'dispersed children of God' (11.52) who are prepared to journey with Jesus to find God even where he may be least expected.

Thought for the day
What does it mean to live out the 'theology of the Cross' – to die in order that others may live – in our time?

Prayer
Jesus, Jewish stranger,
reconciling this world to God,
building bridges to span our abysses of human hatred,
help us to hold out our hands in greeting and welcome,
to reach across the boundaries imposed by culture or
    convention.

Ben Edson

Holy Week and Easter Sunday

Palm Sunday

The Way of Peace

Is 50:4-9; Ps 118:1-2, 19-29; Ph 2:5-11; Lk 19: 28-40

> *'As he approached Bethphage and Bethany at the hill called the Mount of Olives, he sent two of his disciples.' (Lk 19:29)*

One of the central characters in Nikos Kazantzakis's novel *The Last Temptation of Christ* is Judas: 'Judas was uprooting hairs from his beard and tossing them away. He had expected a different Messiah, a Messiah with a sword ...' (p. 396).

In a country under Roman occupation Judas is treated as a second-class citizen. He wants Jesus to lead a violent revolution to drive the occupiers out. One can only imagine the anger felt by the people of that time as they saw their land taken away, their people enslaved and heavy taxes imposed. It is not surprising that Judas and the religious zealots sought a violent revolution.

Modern day Bethany is located in the Palestinian town of al-Eizariya (Arabic for 'The Place of Lazarus') on the edge of the mountain ridge known as the Mount of Olives. Less than half a mile away, towards Jerusalem, is the Palestinian town of Abu Dis, a town of over 12,000 residents situated on the edge of the East Jerusalem.

Running through the centre of the town is a 12ft wall dividing the town into two – the security barrier erected in 2004 by the Israeli government. A wall that divides families, takes land away and serves to both alienate and radicalized those inside its walls.

Two peoples, two groups divided by 2,000 years, and yet their plight is remarkably similar. The ignominy felt by the today's Palestinian at each check-point, each search, and as each home is destroyed was also felt 2,000 years ago by the Jewish people as Roman occupiers abused their basic human rights. The temptation and urge to use violence must be great and yet we see Jesus offering a different way, a way of peace.

The selection of a colt rather than a horse is bold political statement – an animal of peace rather than violence. Jesus sends two disciples ahead of him to prepare the colt – to prepare the way of peace. The way of peace is the way of the Kingdom of God. Our vocation as Christians must be to stand up to injustices in peaceful ways. Jesus sends two disciples ahead of him to prepare the way of peace; maybe he is sending you.

Thought for the day

The way of peace and justice is the way of Christ and must be the way of all Christians. Where is God calling you to seek peace and justice?

Prayer

Lord God,
In you is justice,
In you is peace.
Help us to follow Jesus' footsteps
As we seek justice and peace for all.
Amen.

Feasting and Fasting

Is 42:1-9; Ps 36:5-11; Heb 9:11-15; Jn 12: 1-11

> '*Mary took a pound of costly perfume made of pure nard, anointed Jesus' feet, and wiped them with her hair. The house was filled with the fragrance of the perfume.*' (Jn 12: 3)

One of the trends of the last decade has been the rediscovery of the *detox*. During a typical *detox* a person will only eat vegetables and drink water for a period of time. It is seen as a time to cleanse the body from impurities. It is hoped that after this short period of fasting that the body will once again be fit and healthy for the pounding of everyday life – a contemporary rediscovery of the importance of fasting.

This rediscovery of fasting can be contrasted with the estimates made by researchers from University College London that 13 million adults will be obese by the time of the 2012 Olympics. As well as overeating there is also the endemic problem of binge drinking in the UK with all the associated health complaints. We also seem to enjoy a feast ...

It appears that we have lost the balance between feasting and fasting. The fast is either used as a confession of a past feast, or as a permission-giver for a forthcoming feast. The fast has become the servant of the feast rather than the opposite side of the same coin.

In the reading today Judas self-righteously scolds Mary's extravagance. We too can look at our contemporary situation and agree with Judas' spoken justification:

there can be no place for extravagance when we have the poor with us. How can I feast when just a few miles away there will homeless people living on the streets of Manchester? Judas calls for worship without extravagance or celebration; an austere faith, from which the feast has been removed.

If we agree, and act, on Judas' argument then life for Christians will be a permanent fast. This is as equally unbalanced as life being a permanent feast. The reading reminds us of the importance of balance; a life that includes both feast and fast. Times where we can feast and celebrate but tempered by a time of fast. Feasting and fasting are part of healthy spiritual discipleship.

Thought for the day
A healthy life involves many careful balancing acts. Feasting and fasting is one example, but there are many more. Which areas of your life are out of balance?

Prayer
Lord God,
reveal to us the areas of our lives out of balance.
Help us to seek your balance for our lives,
so that we may bring your extravagant love and goodness to all we encounter.

The seed of imagination

Is 49: 1-7; Ps 71:1-14; 1 Cor 1:18-31; Jn 12:20-36

> *'I tell you the truth, unless a kernel of wheat falls to the
> ground and dies, it remains only a single seed. But if it dies,
> it produces many seeds.'* (Jn 12:24)

It is estimated that out of 10,000 acorns only 1 will grow
into a mature, acorn producing, oak tree. The other 9,999
acorns fall to the ground and fail to produce any seeds –
a very low rate of success.

We can often view a seed in a very functional way. A
seed's function is to grow into a plant. However, I want to
suggest that the seed's function is far more than that. A
seed feeds our imagination and gives us eyes to see the
possibility of what could be. It points to life beyond the
existing plant and releases the imagination to think about
the future.

Secondly, seeds decompose into the soil under the
existing plant. They add nutrients to the soil that sustain
and increase the longevity of a perennial plant or provide
fertile soil for a new plant to grow on. Seeds sustain the
existing order.

I am often in meetings where stunningly imaginative
ideas get thrown about: We could do this, We could do that.
I get carried away in the heat of the moment until a more
pragmatic side of me starts to emerge. But, realistically, how
could we deliver that? But the importance of imaginative
ideas is not necessarily in their final delivery, but in the way
they open our eyes to what could be, and provide
sustenance for the existing tree. These ideas are like seeds.

Barack Obama's campaign slogan: 'Yes, we can' opened the imagination to what could be. It sowed a seed in the imagination of many young people, giving them hope for the future and challenging them to imagine a more just world. A seed of a free imagination that stands up against injustice, that stands up for the poor and the most marginalized, and for the people dying through a health care system that discriminates against those who have the least.

I am sure that many of you know of both local and global situations of injustice. Let me encourage you to think imaginatively about them and to plant a seed of hope that provides a spark of imagination that says, 'Yes, we can'.

Thought for the day
Is your imagination held captive? Release your imagination today to bring God's kingdom into the present.

Prayer
Lord God
feed the imagination and vision of your people,
so that we can bring justice to the people of this world.
Inspire us to bring change where it is needed
and use us to plant seeds of hope for the future.

Justice for Judas

Is 50:4-9; Ps 70; Heb 12:1-3; Jn 13:21-32

> *'So when he had dipped the piece of bread, he gave it to Judas
> son of Simon Iscariot. After he received the piece of bread,
> Satan entered into him. Jesus said to him, 'Do quickly what
> you are going to do.'* (Jn 13:26b-27)

'Poor old Judas.' Every year during Holy Week we read
about his betrayal of Jesus. A decision written down in
scripture, so that generation after generation can bemoan
his lack of faith in Jesus. I often feel sorry for him.

The consequences of Judas' betrayal were quick and
decisive – Jesus' crucifixion and his own death. Once
Judas knew that he had failed and that he had been
complicit in Satan's plan he saw no other option but to
end his life – all for 30 pieces of silver.

Judas raises many questions in my mind. Is Judas a
pawn in God's almighty plan – a necessary sacrifice for
the greater good? Where is the justice for Judas if he is
predestined for eternal damnation? Is his betrayal an act
of free will? If not, is it just to punish him for it? Many
questions raised by one character that cause us to reflect
on the place of evil in this world and a just response to
it.

Reflecting on Judas also draws my awareness to my
personal failings as I wonder how often I betray Jesus?
My thoughts, my actions and my words are often not
worthy of a person who follows Jesus. I know that I betray
Christ every day, yet, unlike Judas, I know that I am

forgiven. Through the consequences of Judas' betrayal my betrayals can be forgiven.

A cursory glance at a newspaper reveals the consequences of evil in the world: unjust regimes, exploited people and abuse so horrific that it brings us to our knees. Perpetrated by people who have, perhaps, like Judas, had Satan enter them. How do we respond to people who have committed these heinous crimes? Do we condemn them, along with Judas, to eternal damnation or do we seek some form of reconciliation?

The needs of the victim must come first but the perpetrator of the crime, the Judas, is still made in the image of God. To damn them to hell without the offer of God's forgiveness is a betrayal of the image of Christ in that person and the image of Christ in all of humanity.

Thought for the day

I think that Jesus, if given the opportunity, would have offered Judas his forgiveness. Who are the people that we find hard to forgive, is it the time to offer them our forgiveness?

Prayer

Lord God,
In a world that is quick to condemn,
may we be people who seek both justice and forgiveness.
May we stand up for the oppressed,
and seek you forgiveness for the perpetrator.
Amen.

Subverting our perspective

Ex 12:1-4, 11-14; Ps 116; 1 Cor 11:23-26; Jn 13: 1-17, 31-35

> *'Now that I, your Lord and Teacher, have washed your feet,
> you also should wash one another's feet. I have set you an
> example that you should do as I have done for you.'* (Jn 13:15)

Jesus washing the disciples' feet encapsulates many of his
unique characteristics. His actions show he is a different
Messiah to the one expected, he is not an all-conquering
Messiah, but one who prefers subtle yet provocative acts
of subversion; in this case, an act that causes us to reflect
on the relationship that we have with serving and being
served.

In this act of service it is likely that Jesus would have
sat or knelt at the feet of his disciples as he washed their
feet. They are above him, looking down on him, looking
down on God. Through this act of service the disciples are
not looking up to the heavens to find the Messiah, but
down to the earth, the earth that Jesus walked on. Jesus is
a different type of messiah, a messiah grounded in
everyday human existence.

The act of foot-washing changes the perspective
through which the disciples view the Messiah. To 'look
down' on a person means that we don't respect them and
yet here Jesus willingly puts himself into a position where
he will be looked down upon, both literally and cultural-
ly. Through the act of foot-washing the one in authority
becomes the servant, and the one who is being served
looks down on the one with authority. Christ is subverting

normal power structures, and what it means to have authority.

Finally this act draws us to the cross. On the cross, Jesus in all his vulnerability and brokenness is looking down on the world, not from a position of power, but from a place of brokenness. A man who ultimately has the power to take himself off the cross and raise himself above all of humanity in a mighty act of power, once again becomes a servant. A servant who has offered his life to us all and through that offers us a new way to live. A way to live that has serving one another at the centre.

Thought for the day

By serving one another we emulate how Jesus served the disciples. Serving should not be a one off act but a life-time vocation. How will you live out that vocation today?

Prayer

Lord God,
help us to serve one another and help us to serve you.
Through our service,
may oppressive power structures be subverted
and people be freed to live the life that you have for each
    of them.

Despair, Pain and Death

Is 52:1 – 53.12; Ps 22; Heb 4:14-16, 5:7-9; Jn 18:1-19:42

> *'When Jesus had received the wine, he said, 'It is finished.'*
> *Then he bowed his head and gave up his spirit.'* (Jn 19:30)

At nine o'clock on Good Friday in 2006 the streets of Manchester city centre were full of people. They were all taking part in *The Manchester Passion*, a contemporary retelling of the final hours of Jesus' life through the music of Manchester. When Jesus broke bread at the last supper the evocative Joy Division song 'Love Will Tear Us Apart' echoed around the city centre. The crowd were brought to despair as the trial, crucifixion and finally Jesus' death occurred. For a moment there was nothingness, a sense of injustice, whilst the crowd contemplated what had happened. Then a few moments later Jesus appeared on top of the town hall, singing, 'I am the Resurrection' by the Stone Roses. He had been dead for less than two minutes.

I wonder how much time we spend reflecting on the pain caused by injustice in our world? A correct and positive response to injustice is to try and rectify it. However, to campaign against injustice must not be at the expense of spending time in empathy with those suffering. It is noble and commendable to try to correct the injustice that we see but we must also stand alongside the people who are suffering, crying with those whose cry, feeling their hurt, their pain and their sense of injustice. In their despair we see the brokenness of the world and the brokenness of Christ.

I fear that if we bypass this stage those who suffer become sacrificial lambs for a more just world. We can easily lose their pain, and by losing the pain of their suffering we dehumanise both them and ourselves. They become a means to an end.

A consequentialist approach to Jesus' death can mean that we try to rush to the future without focusing on the pain and injustice of this day. There is nothing just about Good Friday. The brutal killing of an innocent man can never be just. On Good Friday I refuse to look to the future, refuse to look for the hope that I know is coming because if I do so the injustice of the moment is lessened. This is a day of despair, rejection and death.

Thought for the day

Suffering is the everyday experience of many, many people today. The cross reminds us of the injustice of suffering. Do not hide from it; despair in it.

Prayer

Lord Jesus,
on the day that you suffered and died,
we seek to stand alongside those who suffer.
In your despair, we see their despair
and in their death we see you.

A Pregnant Pause

Ex 14:10-31; 15:20-21; Rom 6:3-11; Lk 24:1-12

'But on the first day of the week, at early dawn, they came to the tomb, taking the spices that they had prepared. They found the stone rolled away from the tomb.' (Lk 24:1-2a

40 Days of Public Solitude was a visual arts project that I was involved with in Lent 2009. The project involved forty artists or members of the public each spending a day in a glass shop window in Manchester city centre. They were given a meal and some water and were permitted to take three other items with them. They were locked into the window box for eight hours and were not allowed to communicate with the outside world.

As they exited I spoke with many of the participants, asking how they had found the experience. Many of them had struggled with the solitude, but had also enjoyed the opportunity to pause in the midst of their hectic lives. We can often forget that there is a very important button: the pause button.

Holy Saturday is a day to pause, a time to reflect on the journey of Christ through Holy Week. Christ is in the tomb, the numbness of yesterday is still deeply rooted and yet there are rumours; rumours of life. It is a pause, pregnant with possibilities.

It is also a liminal day: a day on the threshold of both great joy and great despair. Threshold moments reveal many possibilities to us; they're an opportunity to look at where we have been, but also an occasion to peer over the precipice and see where we could be going. It is not a day to rush through, but a day to savour. Savour the pause, savour the potential and savour the anticipation of tomorrow.

The pattern of pausing and reflecting on the past whilst anticipating all that the future holds should not be an annual occasion, especially if we are involved in campaigning or working for justice. The Franciscan Priest, Richard Rohr, suggests that social action needs to be balanced with a contemplative life. A contemplative stance that means that our actions in search of justice are deeply rooted in a spiritual discipline that centres on the importance of pausing in our very busy lives.

Thought for the day
A field needs a fallow period to regenerate. How often do you have regenerative fallow periods in your life?

Prayer
Lord Jesus,
we wait in anticipation for tomorrow,
yet we appreciate the importance of today.
Give us the ability to pause,
give us the ability rest,
so that we can serve you and your world more fully.

Alleluia, He is Risen!

Acts 10:34-43; Ps 117; 1 Cor 15:19-26; Jn 20:1-18

> *'Mary Magdalene went and announced to the disciples, "I have seen the Lord"; and she told them that he had said these things to her.' (Jn 20:18)*

Mary; Rabbouni. Two words exchanged and Mary knew that her wildest dreams had come true. There he was, the man whom she had seen crucified just a couple of days ago, alive! A moment where life conquered death and hope overcame despair. A moment that opens a universe of possibilities, where our wildest hopes and dreams can be realized.

The resurrection gives us hope, and in a world that is often dominated by cynicism, we need hope more than ever. I believe in hope, I believe in a better world, I believe we will see justice, I believe that goodness triumphs over evil – the resurrection can give us a naive hopeful confidence to proclaim this. The resurrection shows that even in the darkest times God does not despair on humanity.

The problems of our world are vast and without an interpretive framework to understand them they can overpower us, leading us into despair. The resurrection gives us that interpretive framework. It is a framework that reminds us that in both our personal brokenness and the brokenness of our world that Christ brings resurrection. A framework that gives every Christian the potential to live as a witness to the life bringing power of the resurrection.

The challenge for Christians is to live up to that potential, to live as people of hope, people of resurrection. This is not a call for Christians to be naively happy but to be firmly rooted in this world and yet to live with a deep sense of hope in their lives. To believe that whilst the resurrection of Jesus was a unique one-off event, it is also an attitude and aspiration that we bring to the world – an attitude that brings hope.

Strangely, the resurrection brings us to the end of this journey but the resurrection is never an end point – it is the start. It is the start point that we always return to, where hope overcomes despair and justice triumphs. The resurrection gives us the hope that we will see a just world – now let us go and live the resurrection hope.

Thought for the day

How can you live the resurrection even more? Go forward and take God's hope to all that you encounter.

Prayer

Risen Lord Jesus,
we give thanks that your resurrection gives us hope,
hope that justice will reign,
and hope that will see people liberated.
May we be people who bring you Easter hope to all we
encounter,
this day and everyday.